History and Relevance

Howard Mumford Jones

Edited by Rene Kollar, O.S.B.

WIPF & STOCK · Eugene, Oregon

HISTORY AND RELEVANCE

This lecture was originally published by the Archabbey Press in 1968.

Wipf & Stock Publishers
199 W. 8th Ave., Suite 3
Eugene, OR 97401
www.wipfandstock.com

ISBN 13: 978-1-62032-803-3

Cover photo and inside photos:
Courtesy of Harvard University Archives:
HUP Jones, Howard Mumford (49), (67a), (68a).
Used with permission.

Book design by Kimberley A. Opatka-Metzgar
Saint Vincent Archabbey Publications
Public Relations Associate, Simon Stuchlik

Contents

Foreword

When the Benedictine monk Father Boniface Wimmer (1809-1887) arrived in New York from Rotterdam on September 16, 1846, with five students and fifteen candidates for the brotherhood, his chief goal was to educate and evangelize the German-speaking immigrants of America. After finding conditions too difficult in Carrolltown, Pennsylvania, Wimmer, a monk of the abbey of Metten in Bavaria, accepted the invitation of Bishop Michael O' Connor, the first Bishop of Pittsburgh, Pennsylvania, to settle at Saint Vincent parish, approximately forty miles east of the city, near the current day Latrobe. Wimmer arrived at the spot of his future monastery, the first Benedictine foundation in North America, on October 24, 1846. Wimmer's success was phenomenal. A college was established immediately, membership in the monastery grew, and parishes and other abbeys were founded under his direction. In 1855, Pope Pius IX elevated the community of Saint Vincent—which had grown to over 200 monks—to the status of an Abbey, and in the same year Wimmer became the first Abbot. In 1883, Pope Leo XIII bestowed on him the title of Archabbot.

Archabbot Boniface Wimmer received many recognitions and honors for his educational, missionary, and pastoral work throughout his life, and his many accomplishments are recorded in Jerome Oetgen's *An American Abbot: Boniface Wimmer, O.S.B., 1809-1887* (1997). Oetgen published another book in 2000, *Mission to America. A History of Saint Vincent Archabbey, the First Benedictine Monastery in the United States*, which chronicles the life of the monastery and Wimmer's lasting legacy. Throughout its history, the monastic community at Saint Vincent celebrated anniversaries associated with Wimmer's life in 1946, 1996, and 2009.

Archabbot Wimmer recognized the importance of education in his American monastic environment, and Oegten's books highlight his important contributions to high school, college, and seminary education. An appreciation of learning in the classical tradition and a strong dose of pragmatism formed the basis of his educational philosophy, and Wimmer articulated this approach in his much quoted statement urging teachers and students to "seek first what is necessary, then what is useful, and finally what is beautiful." To celebrate the centenary of the founding of Saint Vincent Archabbey and College in 1946, an annual lecture series was established to honor the memory of Archabbot Boniface Wimmer. In 1947, Kenneth J. Conant delivered the first Wimmer Memorial Lecture entitled *Benedictine Contributions to Church Architecture*, and the series concluded in 1970 with Paul Goodman's lecture on *Silence, Speaking, and Language*. The list of the Wimmer Memorial Lectures is printed in this publication, and an asterisk identifies those lectures, which have been published by The Archabbey Press, Latrobe, Pennsylvania.

I have edited the published lectures given by Christopher Dawson, John Tracy Ellis, and Jacques Maritain, and they have been recently reprinted in a new format with an introduction and foreword. The Wimmer Memorial Lecture given by Howard Mumford Jones in 1969, *History and Relevance*, was first published in 1969 by The Archabbey Press. For this new edition, Dr. Susan Mitchell Sommers, Professor of History at Saint Vincent College, wrote the introduction. My editorial changes to the 1969 publication were minor.

As one can see from the list of speakers and their topics, the Wimmer Memorial Lectures still offer valuable insights into Archabbot Boniface Wimmer's approach to a Catholic, Benedictine, liberal arts education which stresses the necessary, the useful, and the beautiful as the foundation for a productive and meaningful life. Consequently, over the next several years, the Wimmer Lectures which have already been published by The Archabbey Press will appear again in a new format with an introduction, and those unpublished lectures will also be edited and published.

Rene Kollar

Howard Mumford Jones, circa 1960, courtesy Harvard University Archives.

Introduction

Howard Mumford Jones was born in Saginaw, Michigan, in 1892. Just two years previous, Superintendent of the United States Census Robert Percival Porter had announced the closing of the American frontier. Porter's finding was prompted by the rapid settlement, since the Civil War, of the formerly vast open spaces of the Great Plains and far West by millions of immigrants and internal migrants. Both the demographic phenomenon and Porter's conclusions about it had a profound effect on American intellectuals. The end of the frontier provided, fittingly, a promontory from which historians, writers, philosophers, political theorists, sociologists, and theologians could gaze back over the United States' early development and take stock. They seized on this opportunity with alacrity; allowing the closing of the frontier to shape their interests, direct their inquiries, inform public policies, and even to give definition to the University Movement then transforming American higher education.[1]

Most famously and immediately, Frederick Jackson Turner (1861-1932) addressed the newly established American Historical Association (1889), meeting at the Chicago World's Fair in 1893, on "The Significance of the Frontier in American History."[2] Turner argued that a uniquely American character had developed in that ever-shifting liminal space between civilization and wilderness—the frontier. His essay, though scholarly, struck a popular chord and helped define the ongoing public debate about what it meant to be an American at the threshold of the twentieth century. What came to be known as the "Frontier Thesis" so captured the imagination of academics and laymen alike that it dwarfed his other major line of academic inquiry, that being his rejection of what he saw as the now meaningless sectional studies of groups of states (New England, South, Midwest), in favor of regional works focused on rational, flexible, and often quantifiable affinities. The creation of sound regional histories and planning preoccupied much of the rest of Turner's academic career. His essays on sectionalism and regionalism were collected in *The Significance of Sections in American History*, which won a Pulitzer Prize in 1933.

It was Turner's second "thesis" that left its imprint most emphatically on academia generally, and on Howard Mumford Jones in particular. Jones was born in Saginaw when it was in its last throes as a lumber town and the frontier was still fresh in local memory. He graduated from high school in La Crosse in 1910, and began his long and varied association with higher education at the La Crosse Normal School. By 1912 Jones moved on to the University of Wisconsin at Madison, where he breathed deeply of La Follett's Progressivism and became convinced that one of the major purposes of universities was to serve as the intellectual engines of state and regional development. For the rest of his career Jones acted on the conviction that academics had the obligation to be useful to the public in whichever way was most appropriate to their particular field. At Wisconsin, where he read English, and the University of Chicago, where he began graduate work in 1914, Jones studied under many of the great men of the American University Movement, who were also steeped in the Progressive Era determination to make higher education a font of excellence in both theoretical research and pragmatic applications. His professors and mentors belonged to that first generation of American Ph.D.s, men who busied themselves between 1870 and the outbreak of World War I doing seminal research in their fields, but equally as important, founding disciplines and departments and giving form to American higher education on the German model, but with a distinctly American accent.

From the beginning, it was clear that Jones had found his métier in the academy. An only child whose mother had indulged him as much as the family's slim budget allowed, Jones enjoyed delicate health much of his youth. An adolescent summer spent working on the Chicago, Burlington & Quincy Railroad convinced him that his future lay indoors, surrounded by books. Jones was a voracious reader and was correspondingly eclectic in his literary references, and his readers benefit from being similarly erudite. Jones also wrote with ease and humor, and throughout his life remained remarkably versatile with regard to genre—but for some time it was not entirely clear how those attributes would mature into an area of specialization. Of course he had to specialize—the proliferation of departments and narrowing of intellectual focus was one of the more striking characteristics of the new American universities. Jones eventually transformed himself into what is rather inelegantly termed a "critic," but that potentially dismissive term misses the point with Howard Mumford Jones, who in reality was more a practitioner of comparative humanism. Consequently, much of his critical work baffled reviewers who were not entirely certain how to classify either him or his writing. Later in life one reviewer noted wearily, "Mr. Jones has read too many books."[3]

Jones was examined for his master's degree at Chicago in June 1915. His M.A. in hand, the path forward remained frustratingly obscure. He published a translation of Heinrich Heine's poem cycle *The North Sea*, edited *The School Review* for the University of Chicago, and fell into a position teaching freshman composition.[4] With World War I raging overseas, Jones joined other faculty volunteers in the First Illinois Cavalry of the State Militia, in which he determined he was at least as useful as Samuel Taylor Coleridge had been in his own brief military foray.[5] Then an apparent miracle fell in his lap—the first of many university appointments that came looking for him, rather than the more usual frantic search for employment. Jones, a sturdy agnostic, would frown on our use of the term "miracle" here. He was broadly tolerant and profoundly respectful of many religious traditions. Like Voltaire, Jones believed that formal religion tended to make people more ethical and society more stable. However, consistent with the deistic tendencies of many of his Yankee forebears, Jones seems not to have felt the religious impulse himself. Nonetheless, it was his great good fortune to be called into a meeting with his professor Robert Morss Lovett and William James Battle, acting president of the University of Texas, who hired him on the spot to teach literature in Austin.

Jones taught, in fairly rapid succession, at the University of Texas at Austin, the University of Montana at Missoula, and the University of Texas again. On a year's study leave in 1924 he made his way back to the University of Chicago in pursuit of a Ph.D. in Comparative Literature, though he never managed to complete it to the satisfaction of the reigning dean of the graduate school.[6] Not obtaining the degree was a disappointment, though not a crushing one—in those days many celebrated American academics continued to disdain the Ph.D. as superfluous. Nonetheless, Jones's year of intense study in the library paid off, bringing into crystalline focus the themes of his life's work: the multifaceted interplay between historical events, cultural trends, and the development of American literary traditions, and, more broadly, the importance of the humanities in deciphering the meanings and practical importance of these elements of America's past. Jones concluded that nothing in America's evolution was as simple, culturally or geographically, as either the historians or literary scholars would have us believe, but that teasing meaning out of both was essential for the continued vitality of the democracy.[7] Ultimately, he was to argue in *The Theory of American Literature* that what is shared in the American mythological past is more important that the sum of the component mythologies of American's disparate parts.[8] Above all, he saw the unifying historical effect of mediation and compromise, rather than sectional or regional isolation or feuds.

Without a Ph.D., but with renewed purpose, and with Bessie Judith Zaban, his new wife and professional collaborator, Jones left Chicago for yet another amazingly timely job offer. The couple moved to Chapel Hill, where Jones was on the faculty of the University of North Carolina from 1927 through 1930. While there he published his erstwhile doctoral dissertation, rejected by Chicago, as *America and French Culture: 1750-1848*, for which he received the Jusserand Medal from the American Historical Association.[9] This book set the tone and agenda for the four books Jones considered at the center of his life's work. It was followed by *O Strange New World* for which he won a Pulitzer Prize in 1965, *Revolution and Romanticism*, and *The Age of Energy*.[10]

Just as financial exigencies brought on by the Great Depression forced dramatic salary cuts at UNC, Jones received a flattering offer from the University of Michigan at Ann Arbor, which he accepted. He served as Professor of English there from 1930 to 1936. The Jones family had scarcely settled comfortably into Ann Arbor when, in 1932, Jones was approached by Henry Allen Moe, longtime head of the Guggenheim Foundation, President of the American Philosophical Association, and first Director of the National Endowment for the Humanities. Over a daunting lunch during which Jones concluded that Moe knew far more about Jones's business than did Jones himself, Moe persuaded Jones to apply for a grant to research and write about the topic of his choice.[11] The application was successful, and the resulting biography of the Irish poet Tommy Moore (1779-1852), titled *The Harp that Once: A Chron-*

icle of Life of Thomas Moore, is a prime example of Jones's continued eclecticism in interests and genres throughout his career.[12]

One morning in the spring of 1936 Jones was unexpectedly seduced, in the English Department Commons Room, by Harvard University. Truly, propositioned once and then seduced. He received two impressive envelopes. One contained an invitation to become a professor of English at Harvard. The other envelope contained a summons to participate in an international colloquium of one hundred notables on the future of the world, in celebration of Harvard's tercentenary.[13] Jones acquiesced to both, and happily accepted the added inducement of an honorary Ph.D. Howard Mumford Jones remained at Harvard, first as Professor of English from 1936-60, then as Abbott Lawrence Lowell Professor of Humanities from 1960-62 and as Dean of the Graduate school of Arts and Sciences from 1943-44. Both within the academy, and in his later involvement with the America-Israel Society and the American Philosophical Society, he made important and satisfying contributions.

As Jones grew older, he fondly lamented the passing of teachers, mentors, colleagues and friends. His autobiography, published the year before his own death in 1980, was full of regret for those who went before. He also mourned the diminished vigor of American culture, which he perceived as having lost its way through a willful rejection of the relevance of our own history. By the time he delivered the Twenty-Second Wimmer Lecture at Saint Vincent College in 1969, he was on the retreat from being a follower of Robert La Follette and had become an acolyte of Edmund Burke, post French Revolution. In *The Bright Medusa*, published in 1952, Jones had argued, almost begged, "I, for one, hope that youth will again revolt and again demoralize the dead weight of conformity that now lies upon us."[14] But that was seventeen years earlier, and in the face of McCarthyism. When Jones came to Saint Vincent he was sadder, more circumspect, and much less optimistic about the ability of the youth to make wise use of knowledge handed down. Granted, he acknowledged, elders have always wrung their hands over the imprudence of their children and grandchildren. But now, Jones fretted, we were confronted with a generation who believed they were entirely *sui generis*, that nothing remotely like them had come before. The dangerous part of this, Jones suggested, was that by denying the past, the youth of the Vietnam era would irretrievably lose claim over it, and that the precious continuity of interpretation and analysis that made both history and literature memorable and useful would fall into the hands of "the John Birch Society or the American Legion or the Daughters of the American Revolution," none of whom were fit interpreters of the American legacy. Ultimately, Jones concluded:

> The lesson of history is not that it has no lesson; the lesson of history is that only by patience and thought do we amid a thousand blunders slowly improve the lot of man. And to the study of man in this large sense the humanities and history must remain forever committed.[15]

Susan Mitchell Sommers, Ph.D.
Professor of History, Saint Vincent College

Notes

[1]Frederick Rudolph, *The American College and University: A History*, (New York: Alfred A. Knopf, 1962) 329-372.

[2]Frederick Jackson Turner, "The Significance of the Frontier in American History," *Writings on American History*, American Historical Association, (Washington, D.C.: Smithsonian Institution Press, 1894).

[3]Howard Mumford Jones, *Howard Mumford Jones: An Autobiography*, (Madison: The University of Wisconsin Press, 1979) 270.

[4]Jones, *Autobiography*, 62-4.

[5]Samuel Taylor Coleridge volunteered under the *nom de guerre*, Silas Tomkyn Comberbache—his brothers later retrieved him, claiming insanity.

[6]Jones, *Autobiography*, 129.

[7]Jones, *Autobiography*, 268-9; Jones, "History and Relevance," 39-40.

[8]David Marion Holman, *A Certain Slant of Light*, (New Orleans: Louisiana State University Press, 1995), 22; Jones, *The Theory of American Literature*, (Ithaca: Cornell University Press, 1948).

[9]Howard Mumford Jones, *America and French Culture: 1750-1848*, (Chapel Hill, NC: University of North Carolina Press, 1927).

[10]Jones, *O Strange New World: American Culture, the Formative Years*, (New York: The Viking Press, 1964); *Revolution and Romanticism*, (Cambridge, Mass: Belknap Press of Harvard University Press, 1974); *The Age of Energy: Varieties of American Experience, 1865-1915*, (New York: The Viking Press, 1971). Though Jones published the books independently, he later came to think of the order

listed in the text above as the natural progression of the works.

[11]Jones, *Autobiography*, 153.

[12]Jones, *The Harp that Once,* (New York: H. Holt and Company, 1937).

[13]Jones, *Autobiography*, 176-7.

[14]Jones, *The Bright Medusa,* (Urbana: The University of Illinois Press , 1952).

[15]Jones, "History and Relevance," 39-40.

Wimmer Memorial Lectures

Kenneth J. Conant, "Benedictine Contributions to Church and Architecture" (1947) *

Erwin Panofsky, "Gothic Architecture and Scholasticism" (1948) *

Gerald B. Phelan, "The Wisdom of Saint Anselm" (1949) *

Pitirim A. Sorokin, "The Crisis of Our Age Grows" (1950)

Jacques Maritain, "Man's Approach to God," (1951) *

William Foxwell Albright, "Towards a Theistic Humanism" (1952)

Hugh S. Taylor, "The Catholic Intellectual in the Christian Economy" (1953)

Helen C. White, "Prayer and Poetry" (1954) *

E. A. Lowe, "The Finest Book in the World" (1955)

Stephan G. Kuttner, "Harmony form Dissonance: An Interpretation of Medieval Canon Law" (1956) *

Henri Maurice Peyre, "The Problem of Sincerity in Contemporary French Literature" (1957)

John Ching-Hsiung Wu, "Christian Influences in the Common Law" (1958)

Christopher Dawson, "The Movement Towards Christian Unity in the Nineteenth Century" (1960) *

Ignatius T. Eschmann, "Moral Theology Today" (1960)

Paul Oskar Kristeller, "Renaissance Philosophy and Mediaeval Tradition" (1961) *

Gerhart Burian Ladner, "Ad Imaginem Dei: The Image of Man in Mediaeval Art" (1962) *

Frederick D. Rossini, "Some Reflections on Science and Thermodynamics" (1963)

Jean Alfred Ladriere, "Possibility and Task of a Philosophy of Nature" (1964)

John Tracy Ellis, "A Commitment to the Truth" (1965) *

Henry Marenau, "Scientific Indeterminism and Human Freedom" (1966)

Gunnar Myrdal, "The Problem of Objectivity in Social Research" (1967) *

Howard Mumford Jones, "History and Relevance" (1969) *

Paul Weiss, "Theology and Verification" (1969)

Paul Goodman, "Silence, Speaking, and Language" (1970) *

* **Published.**

VERI IUSTIQUE SCIENTIA VINDEX

Wimmer Lecture

THE CHANCELLOR AND DIRECTORS

OF

SAINT VINCENT COLLEGE

CORDIALLY INVITE YOU TO THE

XXII WIMMER LECTURE

TO BE DELIVERED BY

HOWARD MUMFORD JONES

ON THE SUBJECT:

HISTORY AND RELEVANCE

The lecture will be delivered in the auditorium of Kennedy Hall on Thursday evening, February 20, 1969, at 8:00 o'clock.

You are also invited to the reception in the lounge of Kennedy Hall after the lecture.

Howard Mumford Jones

Born Saginaw, Michigan, April 16, 1892; educated at University of Wisconsin, B.A., 1914, University of Chicago, M.A., 1915; honorary degrees: Litt.D., Harvard University, 1936; University of Colorado, 1938; Western Reserve University and University of Wisconsin, 1948; Clark University, 1952; L.H.D., Tulane University, 1938; Ohio State University and Hebrew Union University, 1961; LL.D., Colby College, 1962; University of Utah, 1966.

Professor, University of Texas, 1916-1917; Assistant Professor of English, Montana State University, 1917-1919; Associate Professor of Comparative Literature, University of Texas, 1919-1925; Associate Professor of English, 1925-1927, Professor of English Literature, 1927-1930, University of North Carolina; Professor of English, University of Michigan, 1930-1936; Professor of English, Harvard University, 1936-1960, Abbott Lawrence Lowell Professor of Humanities, 1960-1962, Professor Emeritus, 1962-, Dean of the Graduate School of Arts and Sciences, 1943-1944; President, American Academy of Arts and Sciences, 1944-1951; Educational Consultant, Provost Marshal General's Office, 1945; Chairman, American Council of Learned Societies, 1955-1959; Chairman, Weil Institute, 1959-1960; Editor, *Harvard Library Bulletin*, 1967-.

Member of American-Israel Society, Modern Language Association of America, The American Historical Association, The Colonial Society of Massachusetts, Texas Philosophical Society, American Philosophical Society, Phi Beta Kappa, Sigma Delta Chi, Delta Sigma Rho, Pi Kappa Alpha.

Author of *A Little Book of Local Verse*, 1915; *Gargoyles*, 1918; *The Shadow*, 1917; *The King in Hamlet*, 1921; *A Bibliography of Works of Byron* with R. H. Griffith, 1924; *The Case of Professor Banoring*, 1924; *America and French Culture, 1750-1848*, 1927; *The Romanesque Lyric* with P. S. Allen, 1928; *The Life of Moses Colt Tyler*, 1933; *They Say the Forties*, 1937; *The Harp That Once*, 1937; *Ideas in America*, 1944; *Education and World Tragedy*, 1946; *The Theory of American Literature*, 1948; *Modern Minds* with Richard Ludwig and Marrein Perry, 1949; *The Pursuit of Happiness*, 1953; *The Frontier in American Fiction*, 1956; translations of poems of Heine, 1918-1953; *Guide to American Literature and its Background Since 1890*, 1959; *Humane Traditions in America; A list of Suggested Readings*, 1961; *Aspects of American Poetry; Essays presented to H. M. Jones*, 1962.

Editor of *American Poetry*, with Percy H. Baynton, 1918; *Poems of Edgar Allan Poe*, 1929; *Plays of the Restoration and the 18th Century* with Douglas MacMillan, 1930; *Major American Writers* with E. E. Leisy, 1935; *The College Reader* with R. M. Lovett, 1936; *Oliver Wendell Holmes* with S. I. Hayakawa, 1939; *The Primer of Intellectual Liberty*, 1949; *The Bright Medusa*, 1952; *Letters of Sherwood Anderson* with Walter B. Rideout, 1953; *American Humanism*, 1957; *Reflections on Learning*, 1958; *One Great Society*, 1959; *A Treasury of Scientific Prose, A 19th Century Anthology*, 1963; *O Strange New World*, 1964 (Pulitzer Prize Award); *English Traits* by Ralph Waldo Emerson, 1966; *Jeffersonianism and the American Novel*, 1966; *Belief and Disbelief in American Literature*, 1967.

Howard Mumford Jones, circa 1960, courtesy Harvard University Archives.

History and Relevance

Howard Mumford Jones

Wimmer Memorial Lecture
1969

Wimmer Memorial Lecture

The relative moral health of any epoch as compared with any other is difficult to establish. Every age flatters itself on its wickedness, every era assumes that its predecessor was simple-minded, stuffy, or hypocritical, every generation exculpates itself by saying it lives in a period of transition. Examples abound. If one were to take literally the excoriation of the Hebrew people by their ancient prophets, one would marvel that the Jewish race still exists. If one accepted as fact the language of Juvenal or Procopius one would expect modern Italy and contemporary Greece to be human wastelands. The Florentines were not as abominable as Savonarola said they were, nor the colonial New Englanders as wicked as sermons declared them to be.

But there are judgments and judgments. We regard our own time as a revolutionary age, and perhaps it is. Precisely what the aims of the rebels are nobody seems to know, not even the leaders of the revolt. It is, I think, true that a good many stresses and strains in our society are, if not new in character, novel in intensity. Yet the historian muses on much that is traditional in these conflicts. The rebellion of youth against age is familiar, racial discrimination is unfortunately a familiar story, the existence of slums troubled Americans from before the Civil War, and malnutrition, unemployment, poverty, and frustration have, alas! been components of society for longer than I care to estimate. Even long hair, beards, drug-taking, unkempt clothing, fold-songs, and a wandering life are not modern inventions: they appeared with the first German Romantic School and reappeared in the French generation of 1830, as did a drive for sexual freedom. The graver charge that we are living in a sick society is likewise old. One reads in Jeremiah, a book scholarship refers to the seventh century B.C., that "the carcasses of this people shall be meat for the fowls of the heaven, and the beasts of the earth, and none shall fray them away." In the fourth century A.D. the Greek historian Zosimus wrote that every species of corruption polluted the course of public and private life in the Roman Empire. Johan Huizinga, an authority on the subject, tells us that the fourteenth and fifteenth centuries were obsessed by a vision of death, and our own Henry Adams declared that if history has any meaning, it demonstrates the futility of man, the degradation of society, and the running down of the universe.

To living rebels and contemporary nihilists, however, historical parallels have no meaning. They are, they feel, alive now, not in some alien century, and to them the argument seems conclusive that is after these many decades civilization can produce nothing better than the Vietnam war and what they call the Establishment, society should be destroyed and reconstituted on some pattern they do not make clear. The state is corrupt, the church ineffectual, the elder generation absurd. The fact that civilization has produced a great many more things than the Vietnam war—for example, vaccines, sanitation, public parks, art museums, free libraries, and extraordinary technological triumphs like cheap books and telephones—is apparently of no consequence to a movement that has the flavor of a wild crusade. Not that these young people lack moral values; the difficulty is that their moral values are defined, when they are defined at all, in terms of emotion and the ego, not in terms of the intellect. The want of any conceptualized system of what is right or what is righteous, if it places the rebels with the German romantics, makes rational discussions with them difficult or impossible. They make demands, not propositions; and what is even more remarkable in a country hitherto conscious of history, any sense of the gravity or meaning of the historical continuum weakens or disappears among the rebellious. My topic is, then the relation of humanism to the absolute contemporary judgments and the absolute emotional egotism of the age. I shall use the words "humanism" and "the humanities" interchangeably in my analysis, but I shall always mean by them the departments of learning, including history, customarily called the humanities and the philosophy which shapes, or should shape, their significance to modern man.

The charge that a sense of historicity is weakening or vanishing seems at first sight absurd. Every American highway has its historical markers, and if the automobiles seldom slow down so that those who ride can read, the markers nevertheless multiply. We have rather more than the usual quotas of sculptures, paintings, and monuments commemorating history. We house the National Archives. We preserve Williamsburg and Old Sturbridge, the territorial capital of Montana, and Spanish missions in the Southwest, we piously care for Monticello and Mount Vernon, we erect a marble tomb for General Grant and a marble monument for Abraham Lincoln, and the Confederate flag flies in Alabama and the Texas flag over the Alamo. We have scores of historical societies. We have learned associations interpreting the past—the Modern Language Association, the Medieval Academy of America, the Catholic Historical Society of Western Pennsylvania, and the History of Science Society are examples. We publish innumerable historical magazines and hundreds of books in history and biography. We require the study of history in our grade schools, our secondary schools, our colleges, and our universities.

Continuum is, I think, a word originating in mathematical theory and thence taken over by philosophers and psychologists; I borrow it from F.S.C. Northrop and say that we have hitherto as a nation been living consciously in a historical continuum; that is, we have felt not only that we were perhaps the noblest birth of time but also that we had a cultural mission to fulfill.

But I had better begin by illustrating what I mean by our sense of a continuum. Early explorers, conquerors, and settlers were profoundly conscious of being instruments in history, whatever other motives they may have had. The New World was to be won for Christ as part of the historical mandate of the church, and the new lands were to build a new society, profiting from past examples and avoiding historical errors. One finds this doctrine in the prefatory essays to Richard Hakluyt's Voyages, which somebody called the prose epic of the English race. The Jesuit Relations have a like sense of mission, the Puritans became a new Chosen People modeling their theocracy upon ancient Israel, and so by and by did the Mormons. Revolutionary leaders did not break with England until they had searched the history of the Greeks, the Romans, the Italians, the Swiss, and the Dutch for precedents, and consulted a whole library of European historians and political philosophers for guidance: representative instances are John Adams's Essay on Canon and Feudal Law and his Discourses on Davila, an Italian historian of the French Civil Wars. The Declaration of Independence begins: "When in the course of human events" and appeals to historical precedents, and most of that document is a lengthy historical review of the supposed tyranny of George III.

The eighteenth and nineteenth centuries, moreover, bequeathed to the twentieth century philosophies of history that helped to shape American culture. There was, for example, a doctrine of the rise and fall of the empires basic to the thought of Thomas Jefferson and the poetry of William Cullen Bryant, and I think a majority of the founding fathers felt that even an improved pattern of government in the New World could do a little more than postpone an inevitable decline. This was by and by denied by a providential view evident in George Bancroft and basic to some versions of the American notion of progress. Then there appeared a developmental theory, sometimes marked by Hegelianism, a theory that colors Ralph Waldo Emerson's essay on history in 1841, which declares, among other things, that "we sympathize in the great moments of history, in the great resistances, the great prosperities of men;—because there law was enacted, the sea was searched, the land was found, or the blow was struck, *for us*." Later on an evolutionary concept took over, as in the instance of that greatest of American historical popularizers, John Fiske. The generation of Henry Adams tried to reduce history to a theory of physical dynamics. In practical affairs the leaders of the antebellum South announced they were returning to principles of the Greek democracies, and by and by the embattled North went to war not merely to preserve the union but also on behalf of a historical concept evident in Jules Michelet and Walt Whitman, namely, the development of man in a religion of humanity. Theories might differ, but the great legacy to our time was not merely that the life of man on earth lies within a historical continuum but also that it has taken countless ages for *homo sapiens* to struggle from where he was to where he is today.

What has happened to this inheritance? I shall discuss briefly four important influences adverse to it. One may seem wildly inconsistent with what I have said about our inheritance of historical theory. This is the appearance of library books not so much about historiography as about the epistemology of history; that is, the possibility and nature of historical truth. I suppose this stream of thought had its more immediate headwaters in the theories of Benedetto Croce and Vilfredo Parteo; and it is of course true that some of these volumes—for instance, Roger L. Shinn's *Christianity and the Problem of History* (1953)—affirm the validity of a Christian interpretation. Many biologists declare we are living in the post-Christian age, however; and in any event these books, admirable as they may be, do not appeal to non-Christians. Other writers—examples are Maurice Mandelbaum in *The Problem of Historical Knowledge* (1938) and R.G. Collingwood in *The Idea of History* (1948)—raise metaphysical questions about truth and existence; and still others, like

Morris R. Cohen's *The Meaning of Human History* (1947), seem to say that history is the tragedy of man. The problem is succinctly set forth in a sentence from W.B. Gallie's *Philosophy and Historical Understanding* (1964): "...unlike particular narrative statements, historical explanations cannot be directly supported by 'hard' historical evidence, since the question about any historical explanation is not a question of fact, but of the best way of arranging the facts." In one sense these books elaborate Napoleon's dictum that history is no more than a fable agreed upon; in another sense they take history away from the social sciences and put it among the imaginative arts; but in any context, since the general drift of the debate is to question whether historic truth is possible, the impact of such discussions is to weaken traditional views. Doubtless preceding centuries were only given to accepting simplified general laws. On the other hand, to question or deny the possibility of any governing principle whatever is to open wide the door to anarchy; and if scientists can feel comfortable with a theory of probability, historians and humanists might rest content with some doctrine of probabilism.

My second factor is the curious paradox that the success of history has been the undoing of historic meaning. We cannot now follow any such clear line as sufficed for Voltaire or Thomas Babington Macaulay. History has become kaleidoscopic. The enormous extension of knowledge of the past in all directions staggers credibility. The latest edition of the *Encyclopedia of World History* goes back a million years for the evidence of man's first existence and says that 99% of his life on earth was spent in the *palaeolithic* age, and does not reach the time of Pericles for a good many pages. Lynn White, the medieval historian, said at the centenary of Boston College that research in the Middle Ages has outrun most other specialized fields, though we do not think of medievalism as an especially active area. Minoan culture, the archaic smile, and fascination with the puzzle of the Etruscans have, so to speak, overshadowed modern interest in Alexander the Great and the wars of Marius and Sulla. We have at hand vastly more information about Byzantine culture than Edward Gibbon possessed, and know vastly more about European history than did any nineteenth-century historian. We are searching the pasts of Africa and Asia. The flood of matter produced in American studies alone buries expert and catechumen beneath its mass. Of course truth should always be sought and knowledge grow, but the effect has been to create increasing dubiety about the possibility of either pattern or mastery in history except for the specialist in his special area; or, since choice must be made, a resort to random sampling or a rush into areas indirectly related to history. Examples are archaeology, which permits young Americans to travel and do something, and anthropology, which invites or validates Freudian or Jungian theories about tribal custom and taboo, the folk arts, sexual initiation, and religious ecstasy, these to be transferred to industrialized society as protest. I am not saying the formal study of history has disappeared—far from it!—but what has happened, it seems to me, is that the fashionable doctrine of relevance, uncorrected by philosophical history, has colored or weakened our feeling for any historical continuum.

This brings me to my third consideration: the doctrine of relevance. This demand seems to exist in two related forms. The first is the invention of zealous scholars so deeply concerned about the troubles of our time that they either demand new courses contemporary in theme and tone, or insist that whatever is historic and traditional shall be interpreted in terms of contemporary anxieties. In the extreme case these persons abandon temporal perspective and rational exposition for a random discursiveness known as dialogue. Therefore Charlemagne is nothing more than a museum piece, but Machiavelli is alive; the missionary movement was fatuous, but imperialism is an open evil; the fourth Lateran Council is all right if you go in for that sort of thing, but if you are truly concerned you will plump for existentialism, ecumenicism, and the death of God. Every scripture, says Emerson wisely, should be read in the spirit that brought it forth, but this, though an ancient axiom in the analysis of thought, is now twisted into the proposition: I shall make the past reflect my thought, my anxiety, my analysis, or I shall have no real traffic with it whatever, yielding to its desert spaces at the best only what John Henry Newman called notional but not real assent. This curious fallacy is not confined to history proper; it extends to the interpretation of literature. Mark Twain is no longer a comic writer but a frustrated Freudian, Charles Dickens's plots were not assembled to tell a story but to illustrate sets of symbolism unknown to Dickens, and sexuality in Shakespeare's *Troilus and Cressida* is O.K., but when it appears in *As You Like It* or *The Tempest* it is sentimental tosh.

The other aspect of this novel distortion of scholarship is the denial that there is *any* wisdom in history, coupled with the refusal, notably in the humanities, to study anything tainted with the historical point of view. Frightened or concerned for the problems of the age, some persons, including many of the young, refuse to bother with the literary, musical, artistic, or philosophic achievement of the past on the ground that the human predicament is so singular, it can be understood only in its own terms. An illuminating parallel is found in our law schools, in many of which instruction in the history and development of law is regarded as a useless encumbrance—as useless as information about the barber-surgeons of the Middle Ages would be to a bright young graduate of a medical school. In the humanities this refusal of the past, this denial that any great historical style has meaning for our age is evident in literary instruction; and so widespread is the attitude that almost alone among the nations the United States confers thousands of bachelor's degrees annually upon candidates not only ignorant of the major masterpieces of the literature and philosophy of their own country but ignorant also of major masterpieces of the West. There is one mild modification of this generalization. A sort of equivocation of time permits somebody like Herman Melville or Franz Kafka to be "modern," whereas somebody like James Fenimore Cooper and Friedrich Schiller are antiques so remote from reality as to have no value at all.

The fourth element eating away at the historical continuum is patent but requires discussion. This is the whole vast force of modern hedonism, licit or illicit, the legitimate forms being supported by the mass media, which, if they recognize history, recognize it principally as a costume play. It is of course true that before the invention of permanent verbal records poet, rhapsode, balladist, or bard, sand-painter, sculptor, musician, or sacred dancer was honored as the guardian of tradition. Writing words on parchment or carving them on stone altered only slightly this special status, nor did the invention of printing change it for a time. Even after the writer lost his quasi-sacerdotal function, print still implied permanence: in genteel phrase you published only what was worthwhile. Commercialism, however, inevitably moved the book trade more and more towards mass production, replaced rag paper by chemical paper, and turned first the newspaper, then the magazine and finally the book into transience. Today the effective life of a hardcover book is estimated at about three months and paperbacks are mainly sold as dresses are sold, off a rack.

We also invented advertising. The language of Madison Avenue is meaningless as rational discourse, has no sense of cultural continuity, and is cunningly devised to drug judgment. Its usual phrases are "modern," "smart," "up-to-date," "the car of tomorrow," and the like. Its twin gods are fashion and futurity.

For the first time in history printing is struggling with formidable rivals—the radio, television, and tape recording. The first two with some mild expectations are dedicated to the instant moment and to advertising. Any thoughtful person who has had to stay twenty-four hours in a motel where the television is the sole entertainment discovers that a television program may be described as a flow of commercials interrupted by bits of movies and smaller fragments of news. The latter are instant; the former are supposed to reflect or interpret today's problems in terms of present or future stars of the entertainment world, screen, and stage. There is of course educational television, which has its merits, but it is difficult or impossible to broadcast the beauty of John Keats or the wisdom of Plato or the doctrine of the Trinity; viewers want to be where the action is.

I do not believe print will disappear, but some popular philosophers tell us it is obsolescent, and the principal use of print among the rebels is for slogans, broadsides, and propaganda. This last is of course a repetition of a historical phenomenon evident in the English Civil Wars, the American War for Independence, and the French Revolution.

So much for the chief factors diminishing or denying the historical continuum. I turn now to the emotional morality of the day. Its two poles seem to be equality and self-expression. Equality and self-expression, the latter taking shape as the pursuit of happiness, seem to go back to Jefferson's assertion that all men are created equal and that government must protect life, liberty, and the pursuit of happiness. But Jefferson, whatever else he meant by equality, did not mean that all men are equal to everything; and he felt that equality was supported but not defined by a pattern of education which, though it insisted upon the broadest possible spread of literacy and elementary knowledge, reserved higher studies to those capable of comprehending them. Equality for him meant a career open to the talented, not an intellectual cafeteria for crowded and casual customers.

Liberty is now known as freedom; and freedom and the pursuit of happiness seem to mean total self-expression; at least I read on a college billboard recently: "Have you found yourself? Your identity is not something you develop; it's something you discover within you." I might dismiss this by quoting philosopher George H. Mead: "The human self arises through its ability to take the attitude of the group to which he belongs—because he can talk to himself in terms of the community to which he belongs and lay upon himself the responsibilities that belong to the community; because he can recognize his own duties as over against others—that is what constitutes the self." In this passage "group" is bound to be misinterpreted, and perhaps "communities" also, but the word "responsibilities" and "duties" are operative. Philosophy, however, is irrelevant and George H. Mead is dead.

Alas, the decline of the pulpit and the rise in prestige of the psychiatrist's office as an oracle of wisdom have meant that religion whether as a revelation, stoicism, or the slow unfolding of a man's higher nature, is being replaced by a doctrine of man that transforms sins into a variety of egotism known as a guilt feeling and replaces repentance by personality adjustment. Man was formerly a being with a soul or, if not that a conscience, or if not that, a moral faculty; now, though one or two of these assumptions are still formally a part of most theology and some philosophies, the controlling concepts in ethics tend to be the inner-directed and the outer-directed man of David Reisman. The difference between these concepts strikes me as more formal than fundamental. Inner-directedness too often comes out as the sublime egotism of the romantics; that is, emotional resistance to all social pressures. Outer-directedness is so patently a game of social norms unacceptable to many as to re-enforce egotism. Social explanation takes shape as guilt, frustration, the disturbed personality, alienation, identity crisis, and the like analyses, which, whatever their therapeutic value, throw responsibility for oppression on society regarded as mass and weight, not as opportunity or value. One may doubt that Confucius, Buddha, Socrates, or Jesus would acquiesce in this view of the social norm. Sociological judgments, moreover, become quantitative; judgments or analyses of or on personality remain persistently qualitative, and except as conservative or radical groups yearn for "leadership"—an odd comment on their cry for individualized freedom—there seems to be no commensurability in these two interpretations of modernity.

I speak briefly now of religion and with the greatest diffidence, for I am neither priest nor theologian, but only a troubled citizen watching and trying to evaluate developments in the churches from an outsider's point of view. I confess that the churches, whether Catholic, Protestant, or Jewish, in their efforts to adjust to youth and revolution seem to me to put on a little too eagerly the garments of accommodation. It is a commonplace that the church is always torn between historicity and change. Doubtless there is something to be said for introducing jazz into church services, just as there is some distant precedent for regarding the church edifice as the modern equivalent of a city of refuge. Wiser men than I have found it desirable to translate the glories of ecclesiastical Latin into various vernacular tongues. It is perhaps too soon to evaluate the results of such a change. I am skeptical whether these externalizations of an honest desire to keep abreast with revolutionary change are fully persuasive among youthful rebels or among aging liberals. Along with Matthew Arnold, Cardinal Newman, and T.S. Eliot I think that poetry and tradition are essential to faith. I believe that style is as basic to ritual as it is to art. Putting aside the difficult problem of the church's relation to social stress, I feel that since the church is likely to be here a long time after the present tumults have joined one thousand other tumults that are now phantoms in the past, I doubt that much is really gained by yielding to fashion, and suggest that more is won by the exercise of educational intelligence. There are, no doubt, platitudes, but there is much to be said for platitudes, which are, after all, the worn, yet standard coinage of all human experience. I know that religion forever walks the narrow path between obsolescence and reality, and I have no skill to plot this narrow way. Yet I doubt that television programs are proper substitutes for quietness.

My analysis has been somber. To talk modern parlance, is there no countervailing force in our society? We may put aside, I think, the *ad hoc* invention of courses or curricula to placate a student mob, the new left, or the new nihilism. Universities will survive. I think we should view with skepticism the attempt of well-meaning humanists to talk the language of rebellion, accept the transient views of the young as to what is acceptable to society, and retain as students those who have no desire to study anything. Culture is not thus nourished, and I think Jefferson was never more wrong-headed than when in an unguarded moment he said that the tree of liberty must be refreshed from time to time with the blood of patriots and tyrants as a sort of natural manure. We must recognize that we cannot restore the unity of scholasticism nor revive either the education of a gentleman according to Castiglione or instruction in polite learning according to Dr. Johnson. We, too, sit before the roaring Loom of Time, and if we cannot agree with Carlyle or Goethe that Nature is the living visible garment of God, we cannot, even in the age of Einstein, make the loom stand still and live in an eternal present tense.

What sensible philosophical center can be reinstituted in the humanities, on which, more than on any other branch of learning, a healthy republican culture depends?

In the first place the assumption of many young scholars and too many students that reason is no longer the chief, or even a credible, guide in art, philosophy, religion, and ethics seems to me to require constant and patient correction. It is simply not true that either American or all Western culture is a failure, that the rational is always a hypocritical mask for something else, that the elder generation is always wrong, that religion and philosophy have reached a dead end, and that the past is not only a bucket of ashes but also a middle-class disguise for a sanctimonious reaction against ardent youth.

You cannot paint pictures, write music, publish a poem, carve a statue or hammer one together, put up skyscrapers, make an announcement in print or over the air, or even rebel, without accepting vast complexes of rational achievements such as the discovery of gravity, the laws of mathematics, the idea of proportion, the principles governing the way the eye or the ear receives and organizes color or sound, and the remarkable capacity of the mind to translate black marks on white paper within conventions generally known as grammar, spelling, syntax, punctuation, typography, and line, into information, imagination, or beauty. It is obvious to any mature mind, and happily is becoming clearer to many immature ones, that the basis of all scholarship, all science, all philosophy, all theology is rational discourse; that man is a being, if not rational, then, as even Dean Swift admitted, *capax rationis;* and it ought to be known that Freud, regarded as the great exponent of the power of irrational psychological drives, thought that in exposing their power, which is great, he was aiding rationality and culture to protect itself and to develop. All this is obvious, and I have said so several times in other places ere now, but unfortunately the obvious in any age of emotional storm tends to be overlooked.

My next point is the basic value of a comparative point of view, of not yielding in the name of modernity to the drives of modernism. The exploitation of the irrational and the absurd is nothing novel, nothing strange. The first and second German romantic schools went in for this sort of thing, as anyone can discover by sitting through a performance of Jacques Offenbach's *The Tales of Hoffman*. So did romanticism in France, England, and the United States. I doubt that much was added to art by the students of the painter Jacques-Louis David, who sought to reform society by letting their hair grow long, eating oranges and dates, and smoking Oriental tobacco, while, clothed in flowing white gowns, they discussed the Bible, Pythagoras, and each other's work. I do not conceive that Edgar Allan Poe's story, *The Tell-Tale Heart,* is proof that Americans in 1840 were given to murder, nor infer from Thomas De Quincey's *Confessions of an English Opium-Eater* that Britain under George IV was a land of universal hallucination. I do not think that *Finnegan's Wake* is truer to life than Johann Wolfgang von Goethe's *Faust,* or that Kurt Weill's nihilistic *Rise and Fall of the City of Mahagonny* is superior to Giuseppe Verdi's *Otello*, which is tragic, nor do I think *Fanny Hill*, intended to demonstrate in 1750 that sex is just good, clean fun, is profounder than *Dombey and Son*, that record of tension between a human couple, published in 1848, in which copulation is never mentioned. Yet such are some of the presuppositions among some teachings of modern criticism.

We are gravely told that religion, philosophy, theology, and the traditions of art having failed, we must adjust to the modern world and interpret man in terms of a wholly secular and irrational pattern of values. Some departments of philosophy, it is true, seem fascinated by the technology of their subject and seem to forget that the import of philosophy is how to live wisely—at least, that is the motto of the Phi Beta Kappa. It is fashionable to assert that God is dead or on a journey and to go in for Zen Buddhism, or LSD, or pot, or sexual rapture, or, oddly enough, the churches as cities of refuge, the refugees having no obligation to maintain the churches. But if we are living in the wane of Christianity, nobility and altruism are not therefore impossible. The age of Plato and Socrates, commonly regarded as a high point in man's ethical development, was ignorant of theology, and the author of that great monument of Stoic thought, the *Meditations* of Marcus Aurelius Antoninus, a book in its way as lofty as *The Imitation of Christ*, totally misapprehended both Judaism and Christianity. The vogue of existentialism seems to me, on the whole, mainly an excuse for what Matthew Arnold would call doing as one likes. Yet even if one goes all the way with Jean-Paul Sartre, denies the existence of God, puts being in the midst of nothingness, accepts the anguish of responsibility, and argues that man is responsible for everything except responsibility, man, thus compelled to act like a god, is still described in rational terms—for example, "being" and "responsibility," and is not expected to imitate Robinson Crusoe on a desert island but somehow to maintain both society and himself against society. I am no metaphysician, but I am haunted by the feeling that I have read something very like this in Homer, Ecclesiastes, Sophocles, and Shakespeare. If man is condemned to be free in a world he never made, he is not therefore to write on the lintels of his doorpost the word "Whim." There may be little wisdom in the wise—a phrase, by the by, from a poet much touted by the younger generation in 1914—but this does not especially prove superior wisdom in people under thirty.

My last point is that it is impossible to return to humanism as it was. We cannot restore Greek and Latin. The psychology of Jefferson is hopelessly dated. We cannot reinstitute science as natural philosophy. Nor is it seemly or desirable to reverse some of the commitments of higher education to the present tense. Nor do I wish to be misunderstood as implying that the moderns are forever wrong, the ancients forever right. But it is not the duty of the humanities to plug for the modern, or to endorse fashion, or to confuse creativity with contemplation. Their duty is to ponder, to evaluate, to judge, to warn, to guide. I think the canon of humane judgment is neither primarily aesthetic nor wholly moral, but aesthetic, moral, social, and philosophic in the light of time and history. Such, at any rate, was the theory on which the republic was founded, a theory not to be distorted into an emotional upsurge of sit-ins, demands, and the transparent fallacy that scholarship and propaganda are interchangeable terms. The Declaration of Independence, to whose doctrines of liberty, equality, and the pursuit of happiness the dissident appeal, did not dissolve society into groups of alienated men. On the contrary it proclaimed the necessity of government founded on principles and organized into forms likely to effect the happiness and safety of the people. The constitution was by its framers intended to create a more perfect union, establish justice, insure tranquility, provide for defense, promote the general welfare, and secure the blessings of liberty to people and to their posterity. I wish the rebellious would read *all* the introductory matter, and not just some of it. I can see nothing inhumane in either document, and I do not think either the John Birch Society or the American Legion or the Daughters of the American Revolution are proper interpreters of these phrases, just as I do not think the Blacks or the anti-draft people or the Students for a Democratic Society have grasped the elements of either the constitution or man as a political animal. I remind you that if as a young rebel Jean-Jacques Rousseau argued that the arts and sciences have debased morality, as a mature writer he wrote *The Social Contract* as a bias for both order and liberty in the state.

When on other occasions I have uttered what seem to me these elementary truths about the relation of tradition and history to the health of society, I am always being understood as implying that art must have social significance, the artist must take a political stance, and his political stance must be satisfactory to, apparently, Edmund Burke. Not at all. Not the artist but the humanist must understand what is meant by social responsibility. The humanist must remain deeply aware that he is a citizen of no mean community, or rather two of them—the United States as philosophically conceived by those who created it, and that great society William Wordsworth once described as comprising the noble living and the noble dead.

In a free society the artist and the critic are entirely justified in asking: Is this good art? and it is probable that the artist must be given greater latitude than he had, say, in the Age of the Enlightenment. But the humanist in this same free society must ask another question: what is this good art good for? The excellence of art may, indeed, exist as an end in itself, something that may be true of any pleasing or exciting succession or pattern of words, tones, colors, shapes, or thoughts evident in much contemporary literature, a great deal of abstract painting, contemporary sculpture, or the so called tone-row in contemporary music. But these examples of modernity, often fascinating in themselves and sometimes promising to extend human sensibility, must not be mistaken for the totality of man. Aristotle's statement is still just: like it or not, man is a political animal. You cannot found a city or reform a state on the mere abstract doctrine that some sorts of experience expressed in art or thought are startling and therefore valuable. The humanist will never suppress nor censor art; he will, however, if he be wise, range and evaluate the experience of art and thought in terms of civic man. The humanities are, perhaps, means, not ends; but they are certainly responsibilities, not self-expression, an outlook on total history, not a congeries of departments. And I add that anybody who has read Crane Brinton's *The Anatomy of Revolution* with care will look upon the cry that nothing short of revolution, destruction, and re-making society will do with a certain skepticism. The Yugoslav writer, Milovan Djilas, who knows something about revolutions, has said, I think, the last word on revolution as a political instrument when he wrote: "The fact is, we now see that a revolution cannot change a nation, its tendencies and qualities and traits. Revolution only changes the form of power and property, but not the nation itself." The lesson of history is not that it has no lesson; the lesson of history is that only by patience and thought do we amid a thousand blunders slowly improve the lot of man. And to the study of man in this large sense the humanities and history must remain forever committed.